Your Government:
How It Works

How a Bill
Is Passed

Mike Bonner

Arthur M. Schlesinger, jr.
Senior Consulting Editor

Chelsea House Publishers
Philadelphia

This book is lovingly dedicated to my daughter, Karen, who is a most accomplished advocate for her generation.

CHELSEA HOUSE PUBLISHERS
Editor in Chief Stephen Reginald
Production Manager Pamela Loos
Art Director Sara Davis
Director of Photography Judy L. Hasday
Managing Editor James D. Gallagher
Senior Production Editor LeeAnne Gelletly

Staff for HOW A BILL IS PASSED
Project Editor Anne Hill
Project Editor/Publishing Coordinator Jim McAvoy
Associate Art Director Takeshi Takahashi
Series Designer Takeshi Takahashi, Keith Trego

The Chelsea House World Wide Web address is
http://www.chelseahouse.com

3 5 7 9 8 6 4 2

Library of Congress Cataloging-in-Publication Data

Bonner, Mike, 1951–
    How a bill is passed / by Mike Bonner.
        p. cm. — (Your government—how it works)
    Includes bibliographical references and index.
    Summary: Explains how a bill, or proposed law, is created, debated, and passed.
    ISBN 0-7910-5537-X (hc)
    1. Bill drafting—United States—Juvenile literature. 2. Legislation—United States—Juvenile literature. 3. Legislative bodies—United States—Juvenile literature. [1. Legislation. 2. Law.] I. Title. II. Series.

KF4950.Z9 B66 2000
328.73'077—dc21   99-049274

Contents

YOUR GOVERNMENT
HOW IT WORKS

Introduction

Government: Crises of Confidence

Arthur M. Schlesinger, jr.

FROM THE START, Americans have regarded their government with a mixture of reliance and mistrust. The men who founded the republic understood the importance of government. "If men were angels," observed the 51st Federalist Paper, "no government would be necessary." But men are not angels. Because human beings are subject to wicked as well as to noble impulses, government was deemed essential to assure freedom and order.

The American revolutionaries, however, also knew that government could become a source of injury and oppression. The men who gathered in Philadelphia in 1787 to write the Constitution therefore had two purposes in mind: They wanted to establish a strong central authority and to limit that central authority's capacity to abuse its power.

To prevent the abuse of power, the Founding Fathers wrote two basic principles into the Constitution. The principle of federalism divided power between the state governments and the central authority. The principle of the separation of powers subdivided the central authority itself into three branches—the executive, the legislative, and the judiciary—so that "each may be a check on the other."

YOUR GOVERNMENT: HOW IT WORKS examines some of the major parts of that central authority, the federal government. It explains how various officials, agencies, and departments operate and explores the political organizations that have grown up to serve the needs of government.

Introduction

The federal government as presented in the Constitution was more an idealistic construct than a practical administrative structure. It was barely functional when it came into being.

This was especially true of the executive branch. The Constitution did not describe the executive branch in any detail. After vesting executive power in the president, it assumed the existence of "executive departments" without specifying what these departments should be. Congress began defining their functions in 1789 by creating the Departments of State, Treasury, and War.

President Washington, assisted by Secretary of the Treasury Alexander Hamilton, equipped the infant republic with a working administrative structure. Congress also continued that process by creating more executive departments as they were needed.

Throughout the 19th century, the number of federal government workers increased at a consistently faster rate than did the population. Increasing concerns about the politicization of public service led to efforts—bitterly opposed by politicians—to reform it in the latter part of the century.

The 20th century saw considerable expansion of the federal establishment. More importantly, it saw growing impatience with bureaucracy in society as a whole.

The Great Depression during the 1930s confronted the nation with its greatest crisis since the Civil War. Under Franklin Roosevelt, the New Deal reshaped the federal government, assigning it a variety of new responsibilities and greatly expanding its regulatory functions. By 1940, the number of federal workers passed the 1 million mark.

Critics complained of big government and bureaucracy. Business owners resented federal regulation. Conservatives worried about the impact of paternalistic government on self-reliance, on community responsibility, and on economic and personal freedom.

When the United States entered World War II in 1941, government agencies focused their energies on supporting the war effort. By the end of World War II, federal civilian employment had risen to 3.8 million. With peace, the federal establishment declined to around 2 million in 1950. Then growth resumed, reaching 2.8 million by the 1980s.

A large part of this growth was the result of the national government assuming new functions such as: affirmative action in civil rights, environmental protection, and safety and health in the workplace.

Some critics became convinced that the national government was a steadily growing behemoth swallowing up the liberties of the people. The 1980s brought new intensity to the debate about government growth. Foes of Washington bureaucrats preferred local government, feeling it more responsive to popular needs.

But local government is characteristically the government of the locally powerful. Historically, the locally powerless have often won their human and constitutional rights by appealing to the national government. The national government has defended racial justice against local bigotry, upheld the Bill of Rights against local vigilantism, and protected natural resources from local greed. It has civilized industry and secured the rights of labor organizations. Had the states' rights creed prevailed, perhaps slavery would still exist in the United States.

Americans are still of two minds. When pollsters ask large, spacious questions—Do you think government has become too involved in your lives? Do you think government should stop regulating business?—a sizable majority opposes big government. But when asked specific questions about the practical work of government—Do you favor Social Security? Unemployment compensation? Medicare? Health and safety standards in factories? Environmental protection?—a sizable majority approves of intervention.

We do not like bureaucracy, but we cannot live without it. We need its genius for organizing the intricate details of our daily lives. Without bureaucracy, modern society would collapse. It would be impossible to run any of the large public and private organizations we depend on without bureaucracy's division of labor and hierarchy of authority. The challenge is to keep these necessary structures of our civilization flexible, efficient, and capable of innovation.

More than 200 years after the drafting of the Constitution, Americans still rely on government but also mistrust it. These attitudes continue to serve us well. What we mistrust, we are more likely to monitor. And government needs our constant attention if it is to avoid inefficiency, incompetence, and arbitrariness. Without our informed participation, it cannot serve us individually or help us as a people to attain the lofty goals of the Founding Fathers.

Senators in the chambers of the United States Senate are sworn in by Chief Justice William Rehnquist at the start of President William Jefferson Clinton's impeachment trial, January 1999.

CHAPTER **1**

From Idea to Bill

A **BILL** IS A proposed law. Politicians discuss, debate, and vote on bills in legislative bodies around the world. Before any new law may be enacted, it must be drafted in a simple written form. Members of the legislature must know what they are voting on. The idea that proposed laws should be considered in written form began in Roman times. Two thousand years ago, the Romans had a legislative body called the Senate. In the Roman Senate, members debated laws proposed by the consuls and later by the emperor.

In the Latin language, the word *Senate* means old men, or a group of old men. The Romans believed that an elected council of elders was needed to examine laws, to make sure the laws were wise and in keeping with tradition. To be eligible for membership in the Roman Senate, a person had to be a male citizen.

Senators also had to be very rich. For a long time Romans made their own laws, much as Americans do now. After the Roman emperor

Augustus died, the military slowly took over the empire. Laws were decreed by whoever happened to be the emperor. The old Roman republic eventually became a military dictatorship.

The Roman writer Tacitus mentions bills in his two major first-century works, the *Annals* and the *Histories*. In Book XV of the *Annals,* a senator, Paetus Thrasea, speaks approvingly of the "Cincian bill, the Julian laws, and the Calpurnian enactments."

It is customary now to call the simple written form of a new proposed law a bill, following the Roman model.

The Roman Senate is long gone. Nothing like it existed before it appeared and for a very long time, there was nothing like it after it vanished. Kings and rulers made laws that suited them. People obeyed these laws or were punished.

Currently, some of the oldest continuous legislative bodies are in the United States of America. Every year, our legislatures take up thousands of bills for discussion.

There are many other legislative bodies in the United States besides the state legislatures and the Congress. These legislative bodies are local boards, city councils, and county commissions. Because bills are for state and national legislatures only, these local, city, and county legislative bodies do not consider bills when they make laws for their governments. The laws they craft are called **ordinances.**

The United States has 50 separate state legislatures and one federal Congress. The territories also have legislative bodies. Guam, Samoa, and Puerto Rico are among the most active of these bodies. The size of legislatures varies from state to state. The smallest membership belongs to the unique single-chamber legislature of Nebraska, with only 49 members.

The largest membership is the enormous legislature of tiny New Hampshire, with 424 members. That ratio equals one legislator for about every 2,900 people. New Hampshire has the third-largest legislative body on earth, exceeded only by the British Parliament and the Congress.

Houses of Parliament, London, England. The British Parliament is the second-largest legislative body on earth. The United States Congress is the largest.

The Congress of the United States is huge, as befits a nation of nearly 270 million people. There are 535 members of the Congress, 100 in the Senate and 435 in an equal chamber, called the House of Representatives. Each state is assigned two senators and a number of representatives proportionate to its population.

All of our legislative bodies meet on a regular basis to consider the passage of new laws. During the meeting time of a legislature, which is called a session, members are allowed to **introduce** their own bills. A member who introduces a bill becomes the sponsor of that bill.

Members will often seek out other members to ask them to sign their names to the bills they plan to introduce. The signers thereby become cosponsors. Having many cosponsors on a bill will help—although not guarantee—its chances of passage.

Every time a legislative body meets, a vast number of proposed law ideas are presented for deliberation. When a member puts a bill before the body, he or she introduces the bill.

Once a bill is introduced by a member, it must be written up in the special bill form. This is done by a team of lawyers hired by the legislative body. The team of lawyers goes by different names in the various legislatures. In the state of Washington, they are called code revisors. In other states they go by the name of **legislative counsel.** In the Florida state legislature, they are called simply bill drafters.

Although each legislative body does it a bit differently, the basic written form for a bill in the United States is well established. Perhaps the simplest form is the one used by the Congress. At the top of every bill is the number of the Congress that considered the bill. The first session of the 106th Congress, for example, began in January of 1999. One of the bills introduced into Congress that year was H.R. 905, a piece of legislation to reauthorize funding for The National Center for Missing and Exploited Children.

The letters in H.R. 905 signify House of Representatives and not, as it is sometimes assumed, House resolution. A companion measure, S. 249, was also introduced in the Senate. It is not unusual for similar or identical bills to be introduced in the two chambers.

The next part of the bill actually spells out which House of Congress originally considered the bill. In the case of H.R. 905, the bill said "In the House of Representatives" and then listed the introduction date of March 2, 1999, and the sponsor, Representative Michael N. Castle (Republican) of Delaware.

Then the words "A Bill" appeared on the form and a brief statement summarized the bill. The summary for H.R. 905 stated that it directed the administrator of the Office of Juvenile Justice and Delinquency to provide funds for the operation of a 24-hour telephone hot line, to collect statistics, and to train law enforcement agencies in the recovery of missing children.

The final part of a bill is the body, or text. This part can state many different things. Usually it spells out in detail what the bill does or what existing laws it changes. The bill can provide effective dates or give itself a name. H.R. 905 gave itself a name, saying that the act may be called the Missing Children Protection Bill.

After its introduction, a bill will always be published in its special form (in plain English). The special form is designed to make it easy for members and the public to know the purpose of the bill.

Besides member bills, many ideas for new laws come before a legislative body from government agencies. These agencies often have long lists of requests. They would like to do things in a different way or obtain authority to enlarge their operations. Sometimes they want to change a regulation, rule, or procedure. Legislators handle many agency bills, which are part of their regular government housekeeping chores.

An example of housekeeping legislation is a law—enacted in a few states—on how to collect child support from absent parents. Some states do not require employers to tell the government right away when they have hired a new worker. A state child support agency might ask for a law that requires employers to report immediately when they have hired a new worker.

In that way social security numbers of these new employees could be matched against the social security numbers of people who owe child support money. If a match is made, a notice would go out to the employer, instructing them to deduct money from the employee's wages to pay the child support obligation.

To change the law requiring employers to report new hires, however, the child support agency must request the introduction of a bill. They would usually do this well in advance of the time the legislative body meets to avoid getting caught in the rush at the start of a session.

These agency bills usually come to a state legislature as **presession filed** bills. They are generally considered important and are almost always given a **committee** hearing.

Another source of presession filed bills are the licensing boards, councils, and commissions most states have established to regulate professional groups. Like the state agencies, these authorities often want something from the legislature that pertains to their area of responsibility.

The **interim** committee is still another source of pre-session filed bills. An interim committee is a special legislative committee that works on a project between regular sessions.

Interim committees are mainly charged with the task of developing new legislation on complex, thorny, or potentially controversial problems. Trying to make the system of taxation fairer or simpler is an example of something an interim committee might address. The results of any decisions they make would appear before the full body as a package of presession filed bills.

Whenever a legislature meets, the members almost always have a huge stack of bills already facing them. Pre-session filed bills must wait for the attention of the newly elected legislators. Once the members are seated, more bills will be piled on.

Citizens with ideas for bills can have them drafted into bill form and introduced on their behalf. These bills will often carry a subtitle "At the request of . . ." on their headings.

Several other types of bills, besides housekeeping bills and requested bills, come before legislative bodies. Budgetary bills have to do with how the government spends money. Revenue bills have to do with how the government raises money. Regulatory bills require people or organizations to do things in a way that pleases the government.

Most environmental legislation is regulatory. The government regulates how much pollution can be put into the air, into the water, or on the land.

A final type of bill is known as the memorial. These are bills that have no legal force and usually do not require much in the way of trouble or expense. A memorial may honor someone or something for an outstanding act. Once in a while, it condemns someone or something for committing a terrible act.

Congress passed a joint resolution to honor the New York Yankees' victory in the 1996 World Series, declaring October 29, 1996, as "Yankee Day."

Winning sports teams, for example, can be appropriately praised in a legislative memorial. In the Congress, memorials are called concurrent resolutions or joint resolutions.

Once the bill has been properly written up and has at least one sponsor, the member who wants to introduce it must place it in a container outside the Office of the Clerk. Every legislature has an office of the **clerk** or a similar person to handle freshly introduced bills. Congress has a wooden box by the rostrum called the **hopper**. In some state legislatures, the hopper is nothing more than a wire basket. After being dropped in the hopper the bill begins its passage through the legislative process. The clerk assigns it a number and submits it to the **presiding officer** for committee assignment.

When the bill comes out of the hopper, it follows a set of steps governed by standing legislative rules. The first step is the announcement of the introduction of the bill.

Middle school students and members of Congress applaud the Ed Flex Bill's signing in an April 27, 1999, ceremony. Senate Majority Leader Trent Lott is seated on the right.

CHAPTER 2

Out of the Hopper

TO HELP UNDERSTAND THE complicated process that leads to the passage of a bill, we examine a couple of pieces of real-life legislation. The first bill is a congressional act, H.R. 800. It was also known as the Educational Flexibility Partnership Act of 1999. H.R. 800's supporters and opponents in Congress called it Ed Flex for short. Ed Flex passed during the 106th Session of Congress in 1999 and was signed into law by President Clinton on April 29, 1999. As is common with major pieces of federal legislation, Ed Flex started out as two separate bills. The first introduction of the bill came in the United States Senate on January 21, 1999. Senator Bill Frist (Republican from Tennessee) was the sponsor, along with 44 cosponsors. The Senate version was numbered S.B. 280; the House version was H.R. 800. Senators ceased action on their version of the bill on March 11, 1999. Later they substituted the House version for the Senate bill. What finally passed in the Congress was the House version of Ed Flex, H.R. 800.

The Ed Flex Bill was the first major piece of legislation to make it through Congress in the aftermath of the Clinton impeachment trial. The idea behind the Ed Flex Bill was to allow the states more freedom in spending the federal education subsidies they receive.

Allowing more freedom in spending was a shift from past practices. When the federal government doles out part of its vast resources to the states, numerous requirements usually go along with the money. These requirements, or strings that come attached to federal government money, are called **mandates.** The Ed Flex Bill was crafted to eliminate some of the mandates so the states might experiment a bit more with their school money.

Along with the reductions in mandates came increased accountability for academic performance. In other words, the federal government would let states use their education money to see whether they could bring about better student test scores. The states would do this by funding special programs in public schools.

Another bill we will follow also relates to education. This is a state bill, known as S.B. 100, the Oregon Charter Schools Bill. S.B. 100 passed the Oregon state legislature in 1999 and was signed into law by Governor John Kitzhaber (Democrat) on May 27, 1999.

Both bills reflect national concerns about education. There is a popular movement underway in education to explore alternatives to traditional public schools. The movement currently takes several forms. The main thrust of the movement, however, is to put public money into the hands of people who promote alternatives.

Charter schools are independent public schools operated by a variety of sponsoring groups. These schools are neither private nor religious. Their avowed purpose is to provide a child-centered education. In most cases charter schools are exempt from the bureaucratic policies that public schools must follow. Like regular public schools, char-

Ryder Elementary Charter School in Miami, Florida, opened on August 19, 1999, as the United States' first workplace charter school. Charter schools are alternatives to traditional public schools.

ter schools may receive public funds based on their average daily attendance.

The passage of the 1999 Charter Schools Bill in Oregon was a great victory for its supporters. The passage of Ed Flex in Congress was likewise a triumph for educational alternatives. Both the federal Ed Flex Bill and the Oregon Charter Schools Bill are by-products of the effort to encourage alternatives to traditional public schools.

These bills show how the interests of school children are affected by seemingly distant legislatures. Oregon's Charter Schools Bill is a version of other charter school laws, which are now enforced in 35 states.

Normally, when a bill comes out of the hopper, it goes to the Office of the Clerk. Each legislative chamber usually has its own clerk. The clerk assigns the new bill a number and notes it in a log of pending legislation. The next stop is the presiding officer, who will look the bill over

Bills arising from popular movements, such as the Oregon Charter Schools Bill, can positively affect the interests of classes in all parts of the country.

and decide what to do with it. The presiding officer is the one who assigns new bills to a committee. There are a few common rules about how bills must be assigned. One of the rules presiding officers must follow in bill assignment is subject matter. That means the committee receiving the bill must be the same committee that handles similar bills.

The important thing to know about bill assignment is that everything is political. No bill goes to committee without a definite political reason. Political reasons can be as different as snowflakes, but they are always there. The presiding officer isn't going to send a bill he or she likes to a committee that will kill it. Instead, the presiding officer will send a favored bill to a friendly committee. The presiding officer checks the bill and makes a decision—is this a bill that we want or is it a bill that we don't want? If it is a bill the presiding officer doesn't want, it marches off to an unfriendly committee.

"The number one way to kill a bill is to put it in a committee where the chair doesn't want it," said Larry Wells, an Oregon state Republican representative. "That's an example of the power of the speaker or the chairs."

Presiding officers have enormous power over bills. They can do whatever they want within reason because they are elected by their colleagues to command the chamber. Election of presiding officers takes place on a straight party line vote. A majority of the chamber is required to become the presiding officer.

If a party member breaks away from the other party members to support a different party's candidate for the leadership, it causes a big controversy. The selection of legislative leadership is one place where political party membership still counts for a great deal.

House Speaker Newt Gingrich (seated, left) and Senate Majority Leader Trent Lott (seated, right) sign the IRS Reform Bill. Presiding officers assign new bills to committees.

In most legislatures, the presiding officer of the House of Representatives is known as the speaker. The presiding officer for a senate body is usually known as the majority leader or president. Assignment of bills to committee is a crucial job for presiding officers; it is one of their major duties.

In the case of S.B. 100, the bill never went into or came out of the hopper. It was already out of the hopper when the session began. This happened because S.B. 100 was a presession filed bill. It was introduced, read, and referred to committee on the very first day of the session—January 11, 1999.

Because it was part of the legislative agenda of the Oregon Republican legislative leadership, S.B. 100 enjoyed a privileged status. Republicans controlled both the state house and the state senate. It is also typical for the majority party to give key pieces of legislation memorable bill numbers, usually in multiples of five. Examples are S.B. 10, S.B. 100, S.B. 500, H.B. 100, H.B. 1000, and similiar designations.

In most legislatures, bill readings are done by a special speed reader. The reader zips through the readings at each day's regular meeting times. Legislative rules require that bills must be read to the full body as they travel through the process. Because the readings are a formality, most of the time the members don't listen too closely.

When Congress or the state legislatures meet in session, a part of each day is set aside for a "floor" meeting of the body. Early in the session, the full group usually doesn't have much to do. The time of the floor meeting, therefore, comes in the late morning, generally around 11:00 A.M. That way the meeting has a natural ending time of about noon, so everybody can break for lunch.

Later in the session, when there is a huge crush of business coming out of the committees, the full body may meet as early as 8:00 A.M. Close to the end of the session, late afternoon meetings and sometimes even night meetings are required.

The daily meeting begins with the presiding officer pounding his or her gavel. This tells the body that it is time to come to order. The members fall silent and stand by their desks. A prayer is offered and the Pledge of Allegiance is recited. The presiding officer is the chairperson of the floor meetings and the only person who is empowered to grant a member permission to speak.

Before the 1999 legislative session began, S.B. 100 was printed up at the order of Oregon state senate president, Brady Adams, a Republican. From its beginning S.B. 100 was on a fast track to be passed by the Oregon Legislative Assembly. Republicans were in control of the Oregon house and senate in 1999. Republicans in the house held a 34–25–1 majority, with one independent member. Senate Republicans numbered 17 to 13 over the Democrats.

During his opening address to the Senate on January 11, 1999, Adams told his colleagues that he believed that America and Oregon were built on a belief in the power of the people.

"If you work hard and take advantage of the opportunities available to you, someday you can stand in this chamber and talk about shaping Oregon's future," Adams said.

S.B. 100 was the centerpiece of a package of presession filed bills initiated by Adams and other Republican leaders. They were able to do this under special rule because S.B. 100 came out of the work of a legislative interim committee. An earlier version of the Charter Schools Bill had failed during the 1997 session. The Republican legislative leaders, therefore, were taking no chances. They had made passage of the Charter Schools Bill a high priority.

Because S.B. 100 contained a special financial provision, it also had to go to the Ways and Means Committee. The financial provision allowed people who formed new charter schools in Oregon to get public school money from the state. This money is used to pay for school facilities and teachers. In the Oregon legislature, the joint Ways and Means Committee must examine any bill that costs money or might involve taxpayer money.

Meanwhile, in our nation's capital, Representative Michael N. Castle of Delaware and 28 cosponsors introduced H.R. 800 in the U.S. House of Representatives. The Ed Flex Bill was introduced on February 23, 1999, and was immediately referred to the House Committee on Education and the Workforce. One week later, H.R. 800 went through a **markup** session in committee and was voted on. H.R. 800 came out of the full committee on a 33 to 9 vote and went to the House for final consideration there.

S.B. 100, the Oregon Charter Schools Bill, did not fly out of the state senate Education Committee with the speed of its federal cousin. Determined opposition soon developed against S.B. 100, sparked by Oregon teachers' unions. Six public hearings and a work session were needed before S.B. 100 gathered the momentum necessary to get out of the Education Committee. These critical legislative dramas—one quiet, the other noisy—played themselves out in historic capitols at opposite ends of the country during the early months of 1999.

CHAPTER **3**

In Committee

THE SUBSTANTIVE WORK OF any legislative body takes place in committee. Here is where the serious deliberations conducted by a legislative body get underway. In any legislature, members talk about "the process." By that they mean there is a constant review being made of legislative decisions. Most of all, the process means trying to please major interest groups. Much of what drives the legislative process occurs within a committee.

Committee membership is determined by the presiding officer of the body. Generally, it follows a clear pecking order. Senior members get first shot at choice assignments. Political power and longevity usually add up to clout among legislators. There are also, however, other factors that are less easy to define. Leadership has a chemistry that makes certain people stand out and others disappear into the background. With term limits affecting legislatures in many states, longevity is less important than it normally would be. Leadership qualities, on the other hand, are evident at every stage of the legislative process.

Nowhere is leadership more necessary than in committee. The people who know things, who show up on time, who try to listen carefully and ask the right questions may not always carry the day, but they definitely have advantages. Legislators either become or fail to become what political insiders call players. The lawmakers who do not become players sit on the sidelines until the voters force another type of work on them.

Once the bill is assigned to committee, the members of that committee commence deliberations. The first to examine the bill is the head of the committee and his or her staff. After looking it over, the head of the committee decides whether to conduct hearings on it. To help facilitate the work, large committees are often broken down into smaller units, or subcommittees. The United States Congress depends on subcommittees as the source of most amendments and changes, or markups, as they are called.

Because Congress is a full-time body, a major bill can arise at almost any time. Few of the state legislatures are full-time bodies. In a state legislature, a major bill needs to be ready to go before the session begins. It is not often that a bill drafted late in a state legislative session will go anywhere. The bills most likely to succeed are presession filed bills relating to the legislative program of the majority party.

Winning an election is crucial for a party. Whichever party captures control of the chamber will use its power to promote its own legislative agenda. The program of the minority party will receive scant attention. Possibly a senior member of the minority party will be able, on the basis of long-standing service, to push through a bill idea or two. A junior member of the minority will be unlikely to get anything through.

The reasoning behind this is time honored. Legislative leaders interpret the fact that more members of their party have been elected to the legislature as public approval of their program. The minority party cannot make a similar claim. The party platform still means something in a legislative setting, especially when the chief executive is a member of the opposing party. The job of legislative leaders is to advance their party's program.

In the 1998 Oregon legislative elections, the Republicans won both houses of the assembly. In the senate, the Republicans had four more members than did the Democrats, with a count of 17 to 13. In the house, the Republicans numbered 34 and the Democrats 25, with the remaining member being an independent. However, the Republicans had to contend with a second-term Democratic governor in the person of John Kitzhaber, a medical doctor who had previously served as president of the state senate.

This situation was mirrored at the national level, with President Clinton having to deal with a Republican-controlled Congress. In both cases, Democrats held the executive office and Republicans controlled the legislature. When an executive is a member of a party different from the legislative majority party, we have what is called a divided government. Such a situation is difficult for both sides. The executive has a **veto** power over any bills that crop up. If the executive doesn't like a particular bill, he or she can veto it and the bill will not become law.

If the president or the governor wants something from Congress or the state legislature controlled by the opposing party, he or she must be willing to play ball. In such a situation, the legislative and executive members can negotiate a successful outcome or fall apart in partisan rancor. It can go either way and usually does so on a weekly or sometimes daily basis.

At the same time, each side wants to build a package of successful legislation. The voters do not send elected officials to Washington or the state capitals to have them do nothing but fight. Government is a fluid, ever-changing entity. It must be constantly updated, reviewed, modified, and refined. The work must get done.

The only way for the legislature to push through a bill without the support of the executive is to override the executive's veto. Doing so, however, requires a two-thirds majority of both chambers. Although it was perhaps possible for Republicans to override an executive veto in the Oregon state senate, it would be almost impossible in the Oregon house of representatives. The same math applied to the U.S. Congress, where the Republicans held narrow majorities in both chambers.

All of these considerations are weighed when a presiding officer decides which committee will receive a particular bill. Favored legislation gets directed to a favorable committee. Low-priority legislation (such as legislation a junior member might introduce) goes to a committee where it will be "dead on arrival."

Both the chair of the committee and the staff members are carefully selected by the presiding officer and the leadership of the party. The primary job for the committee chair is to get the program of the party through the committee and out to the full body. Committees hold hearings on bills, and witnesses are invited to speak before them. Interested witnesses may also sign up to speak about bills. Before the committee meets, most committee chairs will have a complete bill package they have already prepared for the committee to work on. How well they do their job is determined by how much and how fast the program gets approved and shipped out.

The Oregon Charter Schools Bill
in Committee

Going into the 1999 legislature, Republicans knew that adopting charter schools would be one of their major goals. In making this decision, the Republicans had two thoughts in mind. First, they genuinely believed in the value of a less

Pennsylvania Attorney General Mike Fisher (right) speaks at a Senate Appropriations subcommittee hearing on the federal government's suit against the tobacco industry. Because the tobacco settlement hearings were so complex, subcommittees were formed to share the work.

formal, less-structured education for children. Another consideration was the power of the teachers' unions, especially the Oregon Education Association, or OEA, as it is called. The teachers were one of the strongest supporters of the Democrats. Charter schools would therefore do two things at once. They would undermine the power of the teachers by spreading the job of educating children around and they would also give tax money back to charter school parents.

A May 1999 bulletin from the Center for Educational Reform, a charter schools information clearinghouse, spelled out the case against the teachers:

> [Charter school] teachers are also negotiating performance incentives into their contracts. . . .While teachers love it, their political representation hates it! It destroys the seniority-based job security schemes they have imposed on our public schools and replaces it with merit-based accountability.

When the S.B. 100 Oregon Charter Schools Bill went to committee, it arrived carrying a very high priority. Almost immediately it encountered strong OEA opposition. Suggested amendments to the legislation came from

Democrats on the committee. They found as many problems with the bill as they could and brought these problems up during hearings. The charter school advocates fought back hard, bringing in experts from the charter schools movement. Testimony revealed that while some aspects of the charter school programs were supportable, there were many unresolved issues.

The main sticking point eventually centered on teacher qualifications. The teachers thought it was hypocritical for the Republicans to demand the very highest standards from teachers in public schools and then turn around and say hardly any standards should be applied to teachers at charter schools.

Although more hearings were held, action on the bill slowed down while the two sides fought it out in a series of private meetings. Finally, the Senate Education Committee approved S.B. 100 on a four-to-three party line vote.

The Federal Ed Flex Bill in Committee

At the federal level, a similiar battle was being fought over the Ed Flex proposals in a congressional committee. The money earmarked for federal education subsidies traditionally went to help low-income school children. To address member concerns, a hearing was conducted February 25, 1999, on Ed Flex in the House Subcommittee on Early Childhood, Youth, and Families. The hearing sought to address the impact of the package on poorer children across the board. Twelve states were already trying out programs under a limited Ed Flex policy. The question before the Congress was whether to expand it to all 50 states.

Department of Education Secretary Richard Riley had endorsed the Ed Flex concept in a speech before the National School Boards Association two years earlier. "Everybody likes Ed Flex," Riley said. "It improves education and sounds like a very healthy exercise program, too."

The full House Committee on Education and the Workforce met on March 3 to take up where the subcommittee had left off. The opponents of H.R. 800 offered three amendments that they said would improve the bill. The first amendment said that existing content and performance standards be left in place under Ed Flex. This meant that the states had to follow rules already laid down in their educational experiments. This first amendment quickly failed.

The second amendment would have required states to report to the secretary of education regarding their educational experiments under Ed Flex. The secretary of education would have to inform Congress what the states reported and also determine how reliable they were in their reports. This second amendment also failed.

Interested witnesses, some in wheelchairs, speak at a February 1999 hearing of the Assembly Ways and Means and Senate Finance subcommittees in Carson City, Nevada. The hearing was about funding for disabled people.

Department of Education Secretary Richard Riley, a strong supporter of the Ed Flex concept, speaks to members of a program designed to help at-risk high school students.

Finally, Ed Flex opponents offered an amendment requiring the states to cut off the waivers if the school districts did not improve test scores of students as promised.

Essentially, two things were happening here. The members of Congress who didn't like the Ed Flex Bill were trying to make it better by changing it while they had the chance. Representatives like George Miller (Democrat, California), Patsy Mink (Democrat, Hawaii), David Wu (Democrat, Oregon), and Dale Kildee (Democrat, Michigan) were proposing changes they believed could decrease problems they saw in the bill.

Only one of the amendments offered by the minority in the committee was adopted. Representative Dale Kildee's amendment to "sunset" the bill and provide for termination if student performance did not improve was accepted on a voice vote. A sunset means that a new law stops after a given date and the old law takes over again.

With the amendments out of the way, the House Committee on Education and the Workforce, with a majority of the committee present, favorably reported H.R. 800 to the full body by a 33 to nine vote on March 3.

In this scene from the film The American President, *the attractive and engaging Annette Bening is well-suited to her role as a lobbyist. Michael Douglas plays the president.*

CHAPTER **4**

Professional and Amateur Lobbyists

THE HALLS OF EVERY capitol teem with lobbyists. By definition, lobbyists are vital players in the legislative process. A few lobbyists are unpaid citizen lobbyists. Other lobbyists work part-time, providing their services as needed for their company, union, club, group, organization, or association.

At the highest end of the scale are the full-time corporate lobbyists, protectors of wealthy interests. They are the elite lobbyists, who sometimes become so powerful that legislators run errands for them and ask their advice on a wide range of issues. These elite lobbyists are known to have certain legislators "in their pockets" and expect deferential treatment when they testify before House and Senate committees.

Politicians, often very powerful ones, come and go quickly on the legislative scene. Many lobbyists, however, remain to look after the interests of their employers year in and year out.

The number of lobbyists in the U.S. Congress reached over 18,000 at last count. That means there are nearly 35 lobbyists for every member of Congress. Many of these lobbyists wear two hats. Not only do they peddle their legislative wares to members, they also act as officers of political action committees (PACs).

As a consequence, lobbyists finance the political campaigns of the membership. After the election is over and the legislators go to work, the PAC lobbyists collect IOUs from the members in the form of legislative favors. This same system is in place at all the state capitols, though on a smaller scale.

Lobbyists also attend numerous social functions, mostly to get to know elected officials. Since the beginning of the republic, lobbyists have been as much a part of the legislative process as have speech making, fundraising, and backroom deals.

Lobbyists must be personable. They are hired for their jobs because they have qualities that make people seek their company. It is not their sole qualification but it is an important one. Lobbyists have to be likable in order to gain the trust and confidence of legislators.

Political campaign financing is often arranged by lobbyists or others working behind the scenes. Former Senator Bob Dole appears in support of his wife, Elizabeth Dole, in the 2000 presidential race.

Physically, lobbyists are also a cut above the rest of the population in appearance. Some of the most effective lobbyists are well-groomed and fashionably attired women. The men who work as lobbyists are typically robust, engaging individuals who have qualities of character that attract people to them. This charisma, or natural magnetic charm, is what makes them so successful at their job.

Almost as important, lobbyists have a way of staying around for a long time. Political science studies on lobbyists say that the most influential ones develop special knowledge. They gain great expertise in an area that comes up often for legislative review. They translate that knowledge into a favorable decision for their employers. The best lobbyists can make millions for the clients who hire them.

Lobbyists frequently enjoy their jobs. It is a rare ability to be able to influence legislative processes through your persuasive skills, personal attention, and cash campaign gifts. Because they are so good at what they do, sometimes it is a real wonder that lobbyists do not write all the bills themselves.

A recent addition to the ranks of lobbyists is the citizen lobbyist. These lobbyists are people who take on

Citizen lobbyist Katherine Prescott (left), the national president of Mothers Against Drunk Driving (MADD), watches as First Lady Hillary Clinton (right) ties a ribbon symbolizing the start of an anti-drunk driving campaign.

issues, gain expert knowledge, and craft legislation for no pay at all. They do it because they believe strongly that something must be done about a particular social problem or issue. Current laws against drunk driving and domestic violence, for example, have largely been enacted at the urging of citizen lobbyists.

The Oregon Charter Schools Bill and the Lobby

When Oregon's S.B. 100 Charter Schools Bill went before the senate Education Committee early in the 1999 legislative session, teachers' union lobbyists were ready to strike. On January 13, 1999, two days after the bill was introduced, teachers testified before the Education Committee about the defects they saw in the bill.

Oregon Education Association President James Sager, head of the state's largest teachers' union, spoke on behalf of his members. Sager said that while S.B. 100 offered a good framework from which to begin, teachers were concerned about keeping public funds in public schools, license requirements, union issues, and sponsoring authorities. An OEA legislative hot-line alert from the union went out on January 27, 1999. The alert sharply criticized amendments made to the bill in the Senate Education Committee, chaired by Senator Tom Hartung (Republican). The first objectionable amendment mentioned by the OEA was the licensure provision. This provision would have eliminated license requirements for schools employing less than 11 teachers.

Given the typical size of a charter school, OEA said, in all likelihood no qualified personnel would ever need to be hired. This objection went to the heart of criticisms about charter schools. Many people in the education community suspected that charter schools were an underhanded way for groups of parents and teachers to establish private schools at taxpayer expense, in spite of their claims to the contrary.

In legislative offices and in hallway conversations, the education lobbyists pressed legislators to oppose S.B. 100. Most of the Democrats, who had received hefty campaign donations from the OEA, were willing to agree. The only problem was that there were fewer Democrats in the state senate than there were Republicans. During the 1980s and 1990s, the Democratic party in Oregon had suffered as a result of poor leadership. As the century turned, some in the party feared they would become a permanent legislative minority.

Five public hearings on charter schools were held in the Education Committee, from January 13 to January 25. On January 25, the Education Committee convened for a work session. Minor amendments were made to the S.B. 100 and it was voted out of the committee on a four-to-three vote. From there it moved to the full state senate with a "do pass" recommendation. As is customary, S.B. 100 was also reprinted by the state printer as an "A engrossed" bill.

An engrossed bill is a bill that is printed with amendments. Legislative **engrossment** means "to make a final fair copy" of a particular bill. If a bill is printed again with more amendments it becomes a "B engrossed" bill, and so

Oregon Senate Democrats Avel Gordly (left) and Peter Courtney (right) discuss the April 29, 1999, vote to pass Charter Schools Bill S. B. 100. Education lobbyists persuaded many Democrats to oppose the bill.

on. Engrossing is a way of dressing up a bill before its date with the full body.

Supporters of charter schools had a lobby to help them promote charter schools that was not as well organized as the OEA. Still, the legislative advantage went to charter school advocates because passage was a key part of the Republican agenda.

Once the Charter Schools Bill cleared the state senate, it moved to the Oregon state house, where an even tougher fight was looming.

The Federal Ed Flex Bill and the Lobby

Congressional lobbyists were not very interested in the Ed Flex Bill. Much more attractive to federal lobbyists are bills that raise or spend money. Not every bill is the sort that brings the lobbyists out in force. Ed Flex was spared the attention of most lobbyists because it featured almost nothing they were interested in. One brief hearing was held in Representative Castle's subcommittee and the bill went to the full committee from there. People appearing in front of the subcommittee were mostly a sampling of interested educators.

Among the people who testified were Lorraine Costella, a Maryland public schools superintendent; Carlotta Joyner from the General Accounting Office; Gregg Stubbs, an assistant director of the Ohio Department of Education; and Michael Ward, the superintendent of the North Carolina Department of Public Instruction. These witnesses offered views that were friendly to the expansion of Ed Flex to all 50 states.

Otherwise, Ed Flex escaped the kind of scrutiny a more controversial piece of legislation might have generated. First, the money in the Ed Flex Bill was money already budgeted through the federal Department of Education and earmarked for the states. No major commercial corporations were involved. Any lobbying on Ed Flex would have come from the education establishment.

Ed Flex opponents fought the bill with grace. Over on the Senate side, Minnesota Senator Paul Wellstone (Democrat) attacked the bill for inadequate assessment of the programs. Civil rights groups voiced concerns that the waivers might put poor and minority students at greater risk.

For a major piece of legislation, the debate was gentle on both sides of the issue. Getting angry with your opponents in the legislative process never pays. The person who is your opponent today could be your friend tomorrow. Legislators make sure they are doing everything to get their bills passed. Something they rarely do is become angry when others oppose them. Veteran political insiders try to impress on new members the need to separate the politics of today from the politics of tomorrow. They advise new legislators to push their programs and not let others "push their buttons." State Senator Mae Yih, an Oregon legislator since 1977, says it's about being determined. "Sometimes people are tired of seeing you. Of course, you have to be right. If you are not right, you can forget it."

Right or wrong, Ed Flex was on the fast track to congressional approval. All signs indicated that President Clinton would sign it the moment the bill arrived at the White House.

CHAPTER **5**

Back and Forth

The Oregon Charter Schools Bill

GETTING A BILL THROUGH the legislative process is not a miracle. It only seems so to the people who attempt it. Just because a bill has passed one chamber, the hazardous journey is by no means over. Going into the 1999 Oregon legislative session, Governor John Kitzhaber did not have a reputation as a hands-on executive when it came to bills. If he didn't like a bill he let it be known. Kitzhaber was not slow to use his veto power to kill what he believed were bad bills when they arrived on his desk. Republicans in the legislature had dubbed him Dr. No for his bill rejections.

Two years earlier, the 1997 session of the Oregon legislature had seen the introduction of 3,101 bills. That was not an unusual number for a state with a population of nearly three million people. Of those 3,101 bills, Kitzhaber signed 434, or about 13 percent, into law. He also vetoed 43 bills. This backdrop of a ready veto pen was on the

Representative Ron Sunseri, House Education Committee chairman, answers opponents' questions on April 8, 1999, the day he carried S.B. 100 through the Oregon House of Representatives.

RON SUNSERI

minds of charter school advocates as they pushed S.B. 100 out of the state senate and into the state house.

After the senate Education Committee moved the Charter Schools Bill to the full body, it was rushed through a second reading on February 2, 1999. A third reading came the very next day, February 3. The bill was proceeding straight to the state house for final deliberation there.

Later on February 3, the state senate passed S.B. 100 on a 16-to-14 vote. On February 4, the first reading was held in the Oregon house. S.B. 100 was subsequently referred to the speaker, Representative Lynn Snodgrass (Republican). The speaker immediately referred S.B. 100 to the house Education Committee, chaired by Representative Ron Sunseri (Republican). A Portland area Republican, Sunseri had the task of shepherding S.B. 100 through the treacherous obstacles in the house.

Throughout this process, the governor's staff was examining S.B. 100 as closely as were the legislators. Sunseri's house Education Committee took up S.B. 100 and conducted hearings on it during February and March of 1999. The lengthy hearings on S.B. 100 gave opponents and friends the chance to hear each other's arguments. Few minds were changed by the proceedings, however. The changes that were made came at the insistence of the governor.

On April 6, the committee sent the bill to the full house with a "do pass" recommendation. Allies of the teachers' unions in the Education Committee produced their own copy of S.B. 100 as a **minority report.** Both the committee report and the minority report were printed as "B engrossed" versions of the bill.

No motion, however, was made on the minority report because the Democrats didn't have the votes. The rules were suspended for a second and third reading. Representative Sunseri **carried** the bill—that is, he spoke in favor of the bill before the voting and answered questions put to him through the speaker.

As the bill gathered momentum, the governor told the press that he would veto S.B. 100 unless more changes were made. In doing so, the governor lined up with the teachers' unions. Among other issues, the governor said the bill was too lax in its treatment of teachers in the semi-independent charter schools. The job of getting the two sides together fell to Senator Tom Hartung, the senate Education Committee chair. Hartung worked diligently behind the scenes to effect a compromise. Provision by provision, Kitzhaber and the teachers got their way, concerning sponsors, number of schools, and prohibition of private conversions. Charter school advocates got their way on teacher employment rights.

"I think I have made some significant concessions," the governor said. Both sides edged closer to the middle ground, or to a consensus, which is the very core of politics.

In the 1960s, when President Lyndon Johnson could not get the two sides to agree on a bill, he would get the leaders

President Lyndon Johnson (center, right) mediates as Secretary of Defense Robert McNamara (left) and South Vietnamese Chief of State Nguyen Van Thieu (right) try to reach an agreement in 1966.

alone in a room, close the door, and turn to them, saying, "Let us reason together." By the sheer force of his personality Johnson would wear the two sides down and get them to make a final agreement. Though effective in its day, Johnson's approach seems ancient now. In the Oregon of 1999, the e-mail messages of charter school advocates and opponents burned with arguments and counterarguments.

The heated debate stirred up folks outside the state capitol. On May 6, a reader of the *Oregonian,* Portland's daily newspaper, set off a flurry of letters when he expressed concerns about having unlicensed teachers in the charter schools.

Another reader wrote back in a May 12 letter to say that licensing wasn't the best measure of a teacher's effectiveness. "The nature of human beings," she wrote, "including licensed teachers, is that sometimes we qualify for things we aren't best suited to do."

Yet another reader went after the Oregon Education Association. She wrote, "Does the teachers union propose that all parents be licensed before they teach their children to tie their shoes or tell time?"

The battle raged back and forth as charter school advocates considered what to do if their bill failed, as it had done in 1997. Despite the governor's threat, the house passed S.B. 100 on a 32-to-26 vote split along party lines.

Meanwhile, the governor's veto threat spurred additional negotiations among the leaders. A variety of proposals went back and forth between the governor and top Republicans. Amendments were suggested and discussed at length. Governor Kitzhaber had no doubt that his party could sustain a veto. Republicans figured that they could win if the bill went to the voters. Special negotiation sessions were conducted outside the public eye to determine if a consensus could be achieved on the bill.

"The governor made nine conditions on what he wanted in a charter bill," Representative Sunseri complained. "We have given him eight and a half. He ought to sign it."

The Federal Ed Flex Bill

No objections were raised in committee against the Ed Flex Bill on the Senate side because no hearings were held on the Senate version of the measure. After its introduction on January 21, S.B. 280 went to the Senate Committee on Health, Education, Labor, and Pensions. One week later the bill was reported to the Senate with a favorable amendment from Senator James Jeffords (Republican, Vermont). Immediately thereafter, S.B. 280 moved to the Senate legislative calendar for action.

On March 3, the heavy maneuvering began. Senator Paul Wellstone, an opponent of Ed Flex, offered an amendment designed to address his concerns regarding accountability. The Senate tabled Wellstone's motion on a 55-to-42 yea–nay vote.

For the next eight days, senators struggled with amendments to S.B. 280, their version of Ed Flex. During the deliberations, 38 different amendments were considered by the Senate. On March 11, the Senate received the House version of Ed Flex as H.R. 800. They decided to accept the House version as their own. Put simply, the Senators grew tired of playing around with their own Ed Flex Bill and accepted the House's version when it arrived.

The House had discussed the same objections to Ed Flex as had the Senate. According to opponents such as Representative Dale Kildee and Representative George Miller, H.R. 800 allowed school districts to spend their federal subsidies on children in richer schools while children in poorer schools did without. Originally, the federal money went to the states and school districts under Title I statutes. These Title I provisions were aimed at improving poverty-stricken schools nationwide with the use of federal funds.

The idea behind Title I was to spend money where it was needed most, on low-income children. Title I's provisions set strict standards for how portions of the subsidies were to be used and accounted for by the jurisdictions receiving them. The money was meant for the poor children of the nation, period. If the federal government trusted the states to spend the money wisely, there wouldn't have been so many reporting requirements in the first place, said Ed Flex opponents.

When stripped of their political and legislative jargon, arguments about bills like H.R. 800 become fairly simple. The supporters of the Ed Flex Bill believed that the states and school districts could be trusted to target their federal Title I money for use in the poorer schools. The opponents of Ed Flex had no such faith.

Opponents believed that the states and school districts might start spending the money on more affluent children. This would happen, they believed, because more affluent parents would be able to apply pressure on the school districts more effectively than could low-income parents.

Congressional supporters of Ed Flex thought it was about time the federal government started trusting the states to do the right thing. Besides, all the paperwork involved with taking the federal money made for too much bureaucracy. The state of Georgia, for example, received

Massachusetts Governor Paul Cellucci signs charters for six new charter schools in four financially diverse cities. Ed Flex opponents feared that most Title I money would go to wealthier communities.

only 6.4 percent of its education budget from federal sources. However, the Georgia Education Department had 29 percent of its 332 employees administering federal programs and completing the required paperwork.

Whatever the merits of either position, Congress was ready to side with the Ed Flex supporters, passing the bill with a vote of 330 to 90 on March 11. On March 23, 1999, the House appointed 11 members to a special **conference committee** to iron out differences the Senate and the House still had on the bill.

A motion to instruct the conferees came up for a vote. Motions to instruct usually limit what members can agree to in committee. Most of the time such a motion is a device to delay or sidetrack an agreement. The motion to instruct fell on a vote of 205 to 222, and the joint conference committee went to work.

Conference committees are the pinnacles of legislative politics. The legislation that comes out of the conference committee is sure to pass, so being a conference member is an honor. Deals are made fast and furiously. The conference report on Ed Flex, resolving the differences between the two chambers, emerged on April 21. From there, the final Ed Flex legislation went to each of the respective chambers for a repass and then on to the president.

Other states, such as Colorado, are using the Ed Flex Bill to fund charter schools. Here students watch as Colorado Governor Bill Owens (front) signs the school finance Bill on March 30, 1999. [Oregon needed to pass its own version of the bill to meet state finance requirements.]

CHAPTER **6**

Signed into Law

The Oregon Charter Schools Bill

AMENDED, BUT STILL ALIVE, S.B. 100 won the approval of Oregon Governor John Kitzhaber on May 18, 1999. Advocates of charter schools and the governor reached a compromise. They decided that half the instructors at charter schools would be licensed teachers. The other teachers would be registered, though not licensed, with the State Teacher Standards and Practices Commission. The teachers registered with the STSPC would still have to undergo background checks. However, half of the charter school instructors would not be required to become fully licensed instructors in the public school mold. A companion bill, H.B. 3240, would create a registry of unlicensed teachers who would be able to teach in Oregon charter schools.

"We have what we think is a great compromise," said one of the state senators, Tom Hartung. "The governor has said he will sign this."

All that remained was passage of the registry bill. At the last minute, the registry language was slipped into another bill, H.B. 2550, introduced by Representative Sunseri, and passed instead. On May 25, H.B. 2550 was made a special order of business and passed the Oregon Senate the next day on an 18-to-12 vote. This cleared the way for S.B. 100 to go to the governor. Now that the compromise was achieved, the H.B. 2550 companion bill zoomed through the process at breakneck speed.

The day after the state senate action on H.B. 2550, the state house agreed with the state senate amendments and repassed the measure. It landed on the governor's desk and was signed on May 27, 1999, along with S.B. 100.

As expected, charter school advocates expressed great joy and relief at the agreement. Charter schools in Oregon could go forward, just in time to apply for some federal grant money.

Representative Ron Sunseri called the charter schools breakthrough "marvelous." "I am pleased we were able to make this work," Sunseri said. He added that the agreement amounted to a payoff for the hearings and public battles over charter schools dating back to 1997.

Governor Kitzhaber's decision was a switch from his original position. He had said from the start that all teachers in the charter schools should be licensed, for the same reasons that regular public school teachers were licensed in Oregon.

Until May 18, the governor had held fast to his position. But as the session moved toward closure, advocates like Sunseri kept talking about taking the issue to the voters. They did not want to compromise further. There were clear indications that charter school advocates might let Kitzhaber veto S.B. 100 over the licensure provision. If he had done so, they planned to refer the bill to the voters in hopes of getting a yes vote from the public to negate the governor's and the teachers' unions' opposition. Oregon has a referendum law that allows the legislature to refer bills to

the people for a vote. Whereas a bill *can* be vetoed, a refer-ral *cannot* be vetoed by the governor. A veto by the gover-nor has to be overridden by a two-thirds majority of both chambers. Although an override might have been possible in the state senate, it would have been impossible in the state house, where Republicans held only a slim majority.

Once the legislature has referred a bill to the people, voting in a costly and draining statewide referendum must take place.

Once a bill has been referred, the issue must be slugged out in a statewide election. Referendums are expensive and draining for both sides. Money gets spent on campaigns that could be used, in this instance, to start charter schools; and citizens become divided over the issue.

There were winners and losers in the charter schools fight. The Oregon Education Association, the state's lead-ing teachers' union, was a loser. After the governor agreed to the compromise, the teachers accused charter school ad-vocates of wanting the best of both worlds.

James Sager, president of the OEA, said the legislators who wanted unlicensed teachers at charter schools were the same ones who had voted to tighten teacher require-ments in the past.

"I'm disappointed," Sager said of the charter schools deal. "I think those are standards we should be proud of and maintain."

As in almost any legislative compromise, however, no side could claim complete victory or complete defeat. The charter school advocates got their charter schools. The teachers' unions got several changes made in S.B. 100 that they deemed important.

Besides keeping half the teachers licensed, the unions wrung another important concession from the compromise plan. The Oregon Department of Education would report to the legislature in 2001 on the qualifications and experience of instructors in charter schools. This report would guide the legislators in making any modifications to Oregon's charter schools law during the next session and thereafter.

When Governor Kitzhaber signed S.B. 100, the legislation made Oregon the 35th state to allow the formation of charter schools. What will eventually happen to charter schools depends on the overall political situation. The powerful teachers' unions still oppose them because the charter schools will be using unlicensed instructors. The state, however, is going to go ahead and experiment with charter schools.

In the meantime, opposing political leaders in Oregon were gearing up for the next round of elections. They hoped the success of their candidates would improve their position. Term limits forced 17 lawmakers out of the state house, another five out of the state senate. The political situation was wide open. Perhaps there would be a loosening of charter school requirements in the next session. Perhaps there would be a tightening. The answer would be determined by who won the battle for seats in the next state legislature. Once that was settled, there would always be another school bill ready to be debated by lawmakers.

When the charter schools fight was over, the legislators felt free to concentrate on other issues. At the head of the list was overall school funding. Democrats wanted a higher figure of the state's growing tax receipts spent on schools. Republicans wanted a lower figure. The two sides were still wrangling over the budget as the 1999 session wound down.

The Federal Ed Flex Bill

Compared to the state charter schools fight, H.R. 800 faced pretty smooth sailing. On April 21, the U.S. House of Representatives agreed to the conference report on a 368-to-57 yea–nay vote. Later that same day, H.R. 800 breezed through the Senate on a 98-to-1 vote. Only Minnesota Senator Paul Wellstone remained opposed to H.R. 800 in its final form, saying he could not support a school measure that provided for so little accountability.

Calling his nay vote a vote of conscience, Wellstone said Ed Flex was a "retreat from our nation's historic commitment to our poorest and most vulnerable children." In his pointed comments against the bill, Wellstone cited the lack of accountability and the lack of sufficient data from the states in which Ed Flex was already being tested.

A vote like Wellstone's takes a great deal of fortitude. A vote cast in opposition to every one of your colleagues is unnerving because people remember something like that. If Wellstone had concerned himself much about conventional wisdom, however, the former Carleton College instructor would never have run against and defeated Rudy Boschwitz in 1990.

After the Ed Flex vote, President Clinton took the opportunity to sign the bill in a special Rose Garden ceremony. About a dozen lawmakers attended on behalf of Congress.

The Ed Flex Bill gave the president a platform on which to showcase a rare instance of bipartisanship. Cooperation between the Democratic and Republican parties had been notably absent in the 106th Congress. Things got so bad that the president faced impeachment over a personal scandal. In contrast, large majorities in both parties were now supporting Ed Flex. President Clinton wanted to

President Clinton signs the Ed Flex Bill on April 29, 1999, in a special Rose Garden ceremony. Lawmakers who worked to pass the bill stand behind him.

extract as much goodwill as he could from the successful passage of a major bill. H.R. 800 gave Clinton the chance to do just that.

"You know, there have been days in the last few years when I'm not sure we could have gotten this many members of Congress to agree that today is Thursday," Clinton joked. "I hope now we're getting off to a good start and we'll keep on doing this."

The initial sponsor of the legislation, Representative Michael Castle, echoed Clinton's sentiments in favor of party cooperation. "We must continue along this path," Castle said.

At the same time, Clinton said he was ready to back away from Ed Flex if the legislation did not work as promised. The arguments Senator Wellstone used against the bill must have been on the president's mind as he spoke.

If the states and school districts do not use the law to produce accountable ends, the president said, "and the money's being misspent under this law, then we'll revert to another system."

The underlying theory behind Ed Flex was to allow more local control of the $11 billion in education subsidies the federal government gives to the states. How well that local control would work out in reality was an unknown factor. The teachers' unions remained unconvinced, but Congress wanted to give it a shot.

The lawmakers who supported Ed Flex were hopeful of success. Representative J. C. Watts Jr., an Oklahoma Republican, said that trusting the people was a better way to go than relying on big government.

"I urge President Clinton and his colleagues in Congress to help us eliminate the federal middleman in Washington and empower our teachers and parents to improve education at the local level," Watts said.

Ed Flex became Public Law No. 106-25 and would be recorded in the federal registries. Very few bills are so successful as Ed Flex. Failed bills outnumber successful bills by about a nine-to-one margin in state legislatures and the Congress. Both Oregon's S.B. 100 and the federal H.R. 800 were unusual in making it through the process. Although it had managed to pass, Oregon's S.B. 100 had much tougher sledding than did federal H.R. 800. Both bills are instructive for showing how the give-and-take of legislative politics forges a consensus.

Easy bills like H.R. 800 make it through with few changes. Hard bills like S.B. 100 end up heavily amended. Our system may not be perfect, but it is good at hammering out a product everyone can live with—at least until the next election comes along.

By the summer of 1999, Republicans in the U.S. House of Representatives were clinging to a 222-to-211 lead over the Democrats, with one vacancy and one independent member. With Ed Flex out of the way, the House of Representatives became embroiled in a fight over a major tax-cut bill. According to the U.S. Constitution, all taxation bills must originate in the House.

One thing can truly be said about our elected officials in Washington: whenever big money is on the line, the lawmakers get tough. The debate over H.R. 800 would seem like a waltz compared to a tax bill. As the summer of 1999 wore on, House Republicans passed a bill for a $792 billion reduction in federal taxes. Clinton-led Democrats countered with a more modest $250 billion cut. Around the capitol, lobbyists poured out of their offices, each seeking their cut of federal dollars.

So it goes with bills. The life of any bill is closely tied to the politics of the moment. Many factors contribute to the success of a bill. An important factor is whether our elected officials believe people will support it. On that count, it has become much easier for them to hear from us. E-mail messages can now fly to our elected officials. Likewise, widespread access to the Internet has made bill information easily available to anyone with a personal

Senate Majority Leader Trent Lott talks about possible political implications for the supporters of a controversial gun control bill. Even if the bill becomes law, the American people have the means to counteract it if they continue to oppose it.

computer. For example, the status of bills before Congress can now be viewed online. Each state legislature also has an Internet access site.

Thanks to the ongoing revolution in information processing, the work of our legislators is less mysterious than ever before. Lawmakers want to pass popular bills because good laws enhance their prestige and keep them in office. Unpopular laws, on the other hand, mean trouble.

If, however, an unpopular bill makes it into law and upsets the people, all is not lost. We can always put new people in office who will pass bills that we, the people, prefer. This has happened in the past and it will happen again in the future. Legislatures are a marketplace of governmental ideas. They are the laboratories of political experiment, especially at the state level. What we know for sure is that if a bill didn't pass this time around, it can always be introduced again the next time the body meets.

Glossary

Bill—A proposed law that comes before a legislative body.

Carrier—The legislator who speaks in favor of a bill when it comes up for a vote.

Charter school—A public school funded by the taxpayers outside of the regular school system.

Clerk—The person in a legislative chamber responsible for handling bills for the members.

Committee—Part of a legislative body that considers bills in a certain subject area; for example, tax bills go to the Ways and Means Committee.

Conference committee—A special legislative committee appointed to iron out differences between versions of a bill that has passed both chambers.

Engrossment—The reprinting of a bill with amendments added to signify to legislators that changes have been made.

Hopper—Any desk or area near the clerk that is set aside for the introduction of new bills in a legislative chamber.

Interim—The time between two legislative sessions.

Introduce—To propose a new law, resolution, or memorial to a legislative body for possible enactment.

Legislative counsel—The lawyers who write up bills in language appropriate to new legislation; also called bill drafters or revisors.

Mandates—Requirements insisted upon by the federal government for money it gives to the states to fund various programs.

Markup—The process of amending a bill in a federal committee or subcommittee.

Minority report—A committee report coming from at least two members that offers an alternative to the majority's position.

Ordinances—Laws passed by jurisdictions smaller than a state, commonwealth, territory, or nation. In most cases ordinances are the laws passed by cities or counties.

Presession filed—A bill that has been introduced before the start of a legislative session; usually reserved for major bills at the state level.

Presiding officer—The leader of a legislative chamber, either the speaker of the house or the Senate president in most cases.

Veto—An action by an executive in disapproval of a bill that has passed both chambers.

Further Reading

Carey, John M. *Term Limits in State Legislatures.* Ann Arbor: University of Michigan Press, 1999.

Fireside, Bryna J., and Levine, Abby. *Is There a Woman in the House . . . or Senate?* Morton Grove, IL: Albert Whitman, 1993.

Heath, David. *Elections in the United States.* Mankato, MN: Capstone Press, 1999.

Heider, Douglas, and Dietz, David. *Legislative Perspectives: A 150 Year History of the Oregon Legislatures from 1843 to 1993.* Portland, OR: Oregon Historical Society Press, 1995.

Lindop, Edmund. *Political Parties.* Brookfield, CT: Twenty-First Century Books, 1996.

Neal, Tommy. *Lawmaking and the Legislative Process: Committees, Connections, and Compromises.* Phoenix, AZ: Oryx Press, 1996.

Schroeder, Patricia. *24 Years of Housework . . . and the Place Is Still a Mess: My Life in Politics.* Kansas City, MO: Andrews McNeel, 1998.

Thro, Ellen. *Twentieth-Century Women Politicians.* New York: Facts on File, 1998.

Website

The status of bills before Congress can be viewed through the Thomas system at http://thomas.loc.gov

Index

ABOUT THE AUTHOR: Mike Bonner is the author of many books for school children. In 1986 Bonner won election to the Metropolitan Service District Council, the regional government covering the Portland, Oregon, area. During the 1980s, Bonner spent two sessions serving as a legislative assistant in the Oregon House of Representatives. He has worked on dozens of political campaigns, beginning as a student volunteer for legendary Oregon Senator Wayne Morse. In 1993 Bonner was elected county chair of his political party, a post he held until 1995.

A graduate of the University of Oregon with a degree in political science, Bonner currently lives in Eugene, Oregon. He is married to Carol Kleinheksel. Mike and Carol have a daughter, Karen, who attends public middle school.

SENIOR CONSULTING EDITOR Arthur M. Schlesinger, jr. is the leading American historian of our time. He won the Pulitzer Prize for his book *The Age of Jackson* (1945) and again for *A Thousand Days* (1965). This chronicle of the Kennedy Administration also won a National Book Award. Professor Schlesinger is the Albert Schweitzer Professor of the Humanities at the City University of New York, and has been involved in several other Chelsea House projects, including the REVOLUTIONARY WAR LEADERS and COLONIAL LEADERS series.

Picture Credits